An Artists Album

M. B. Goffstein

AN ARTISTS
ALBUM

Harper & Row, Publishers

NEW YORK

An Artists Album
Copyright © 1985 by M. B. Goffstein
Printed in the U.S.A. All rights reserved.

Library of Congress Cataloging in Publication Data
Goffstein, M. B.
    An artists album.

    "A Charlotte Zolotow book."
    Summary: Presents brief biographies of the artists
Vermeer, Boudin, Cézanne, Monet and the Woodland Indians
and includes examples of their works.
    1. Art appreciation.   2. Artists—Biography.
[1. Artists.   2. Art appreciation]   I. Title.
N7477.G64 1985   759.4 [B] [920]   85-42612
ISBN 0-06-021994-7
ISBN 0-06-021995-5 (lib. bdg.)

Designed by Constance Fogler
1 2 3 4 5 6 7 8 9 10
First Edition

To David

Contents

Johannes Vermeer

1632-1675

Johannes Vermeer, *View of Delft*, circa 1660
Oil on canvas, 38½ × 46¼ inches (98 × 117.5 cm)
Mauritshuis, The Hague

When you know it,

the sound of his name

strikes a golden tone:

Vermeer.

He lived in Delft,

a place made magic

by his own view

of a red, yellow, blue town

crusted with sugar,

pearls, or salt,

which no rainy gray cloud

could ever dissolve.

Closer at hand,

in *The Little Street,*

as each red brick

has its own place,

and each old woman

her job to do well,

the colored brushstrokes

of Vermeer

build a solid world

that is spacious,

light-filled,

calm, and beautiful.

Delft was known

for blue-and-white pottery—

tiles and dishware.

From Gouda came cheese

and Catharina Bolnes,

Vermeer's wife.

Of eleven children,

did the six daughters

model for their father?

We see girls

with their features

on the streets of New York.

Are they descendents

of Vermeer?

His thirty-five or so

known pictures

are like patterns

in the Oriental rugs

he painted,

new and nappy

at that time,

with haloed dust specks.

The more worn they are,

the clearer they become.

Johannes Vermeer, *Woman Putting on Pearls*, circa 1662
Oil on canvas, 21½ × 17¾ inches (55 × 45 cm)
Bildarchiv Preussischer Kulturbesitz, West Berlin

Eugène Boudin

1824-1898

Eugène Boudin, *Approaching Storm*, 1864
Oil on panel, 14⅜ × 22¾ inches (36.5 × 58 cm)
The Art Institute of Chicago
Gift of Annie Swan Coburn to The Coburn Memorial Collection

In an auction room,

a circle cut

in the stage floor

turns

as the auctioneer calls out

the number of a "lot."

A wooden easel on it

rides around and stops.

It's holding a small painting.

Numbers bounce

about the room,

always going higher.

"Fair warning,"
calls the auctioneer,
and brings his gavel
down.
Someone lucky
owns the painting.
But what of the poor,
color-spotted soul,
the painter,
dead one hundred years?
Don't feel sorry for him—
he had all the fun.

Boudin

"must have been an angel,"

said Courbet,

"to know the skies

so well."

But he was something better.

He was the last

in a long line

of Norman sailors,

and he was bound to paint

their contemplation

of the sea and sky.

At work at the beach,

beneath an umbrella,

in a way, he was an angel.

He taught Claude Monet

to paint from nature.

Neither one

came from Heaven,

but from towns

ringed around

with white canvas wings:

the ports of Le Havre

and Honfleur.

Eugène Boudin, *Three Fishermen*, date unknown
Charcoal, 8⅝ × 10¾ inches (21.9 × 27.2 cm)
Louvre, Cabinet des dessins
Cliché des Musées Nationaux, Paris

The Woodland Indians

Circa 1890-1940

Woodland Indian Woman, *Doll*, circa 1890
Buckskin and cloth, approximately 12 inches tall (30.5 cm)
Photograph by M. B. Goffstein

I photographed
this Woodland Indian doll
very fast
through a glass
in a place
I don't recall.
You can see the beads
I wore
reflected at the upper left;
and that white line's
my camera chain
mirrored
on her friendly face.

For many years

this portrait

has hung alone

above my desk,

and I often wonder:

what is that distortion

in the bottom right-hand

corner?

I remember her "seed beads"

as turquoise-color,

her blouse as indigo blue.

I know her hair

came from a horse.

Her shining eyes

are "pony beads."

Only her tanned skin

could have been made

before the Europeans came.

And look

at her crooked smile.

She's heard lies.

She's seen starvation.

She misses the herds
of buffalo
on the prairie.
She holds the soul
of the woman
who made her and said:
"Be happy!
Carry few possessions,
go lightly,
and look around
in wonder,
while on the earth
as its guest."

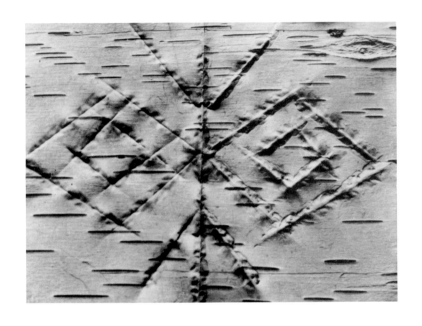

Ojibwa Woman, *Geometric Design*, circa 1940
Birchbark, folded and bitten, approximately 2½ × 4 inches (6.5 × 10 cm)
Milwaukee Public Museum of Milwaukee County

Paul Cézanne

1839-1906

Paul Cézanne, *Pines and Rocks*, 1896–1899
Oil on canvas, 32 × 25¾ inches (81.3 × 65.4 cm)
The Museum of Modern Art, New York
Lillie P. Bliss Collection

A great painting

in a great museum,

regardless of its subject,

is a portrait

of the artist

who, like a child,

gave his whole heart

to the project,

and in the end

knew disappointment

when his skill

could not match his dream.

So he began again,

and he began again.

And he began again

until he could no longer

hold a brush.

A great painting

in a great museum,

regardless of the artist,

is a picture

of some time that's past.

Cézanne set apples

on a plate,

arranged a napkin,

but he did not sit

and eat.

He stared, and thought,

and slowly painted

what he saw:

shreds of colored air.

But not at all calmly!

Feeling dizzy and sick,

his legs like jelly,

when he looked in the mirror,

he saw a stranger.

He had reason

to leave Paris,

to stay in his hometown,

Aix-en-Provence.

As he loved the mountain

Sainte-Victoire,

he endured the hatred

of his neighbors.

For beside the dream

in his own mind,

a great artist

dies a failure.

Paul Cézanne, *Objects on a Washstand*, 1879–1882
Pencil, 4⅞ × 8⅝ inches (12.4 × 21.9 cm)
Courtesy of John Rewald, New York

Claude Monet

1840-1926

Claude Monet, *Water Lilies*, 1905
Oil on canvas, 35¼ × 39¼ inches (89.5 × 100 cm)
Museum of Fine Arts, Boston
Gift of Edward Jackson Holmes

In your straw hat,

white beard,

your tweed suit,

neat boots,

on the wooden bridge

above

the water lilies,

or before

the flower beds

at Giverny,

how we love you,

Claude Monet!

We guard your image

in our minds

the way the poet

Mallarmé

tightly held

the small painting

you gave him,

past Versailles,

past Chartres Cathedral

through the fields,

in the train back to Paris

from your home.

Master of the sunny day,

of snow,

and locomotive smoke,

enveloped

in the scent

of turpentine and oil,

you demanded

that we see

both the pigment

and a flower,

in painted air

and painted water.

You gave artists

new faith

in their brushes, paints,

and rags.

Loving flowers, you gardened

water and land.

Above your round palette,

big and balanced

as a boat,

you might have been a frog

taking in the view

from a lily pad.

Nickolas Muray, *Claude Monet at Giverny*, 1926
Photograph, contact print, 8 × 10 inches (20 × 25.4 cm)
International Museum of Photography at George Eastman House
Rochester, New York